MAN-MADE D
CHERNOBYL

by Nikole Brooks Bethea

Ideas for Parents and Teachers

Pogo Books let children practice reading informational text while introducing them to nonfiction features such as headings, labels, sidebars, maps, and diagrams, as well as a table of contents, glossary, and index.

Carefully leveled text with a strong photo match offers early fluent readers the support they need to succeed.

Before Reading

- "Walk" through the book and point out the various nonfiction features. Ask the student what purpose each feature serves.
- Look at the glossary together. Read and discuss the words.

Read the Book

- Have the child read the book independently.
- Invite him or her to list questions that arise from reading.

After Reading

- Discuss the child's questions. Talk about how he or she might find answers to those questions.
- Prompt the child to think more. Ask: Did you know about Chernobyl before reading this book? What more do you want to learn after reading it?

Pogo Books are published by Jump!
5357 Penn Avenue South
Minneapolis, MN 55419
www.jumplibrary.com

Library of Congress Cataloging-in-Publication Data

Names: Bethea, Nikole Brooks, author.
Title: Chernobyl / by Nikole Brooks Bethea.
Description: Minneapolis, MN: Jump!, Inc., [2018]
Series: Man-made disasters | Audience: Ages 7-10.
Includes bibliographical references and index.
Identifiers: LCCN 2017025701 (print)
LCCN 2017028558 (ebook)
ISBN 9781624967023 (ebook)
ISBN 9781620319161 (hardcover: alk. paper)
ISBN 9781620319178 (pbk.)
Subjects: LCSH: Chernobyl Nuclear Accident, Chornobyl, Ukraine, 1986—Juvenile literature. | Nuclear power plants—Accidents—Ukraine—Chornobyl—Juvenile literature. | Environmental disasters—Ukraine—Chornobyl—Juvenile literature.
Classification: LCC TK1362.U38 (ebook) | LCC TK1362.U38 B486 2018 (print) | DDC 363.17/99094777—dc23
LC record available at https://lccn.loc.gov/2017025701

Editor: Kristine Spanier
Book Designer: Michelle Sonnek
Photo Researcher: Michelle Sonnek

Photo Credits: Shu Ba/Shutterstock, cover (foreground); kpzfoto/Alamy Stock Photo, cover (background), 18-19; Milosz Maslanka/Shutterstock, 1; freelanceartist/Shutterstock, 3 (background); Hintau Aliaksei/Shutterstock, 4 (background); SVF2/Getty Images, 4 (foreground); SSvyat/Shutterstock, 5; Karen Kasmauski/Superstock, 6-7; Sergey Kamshylin/Shutterstock, 8-9; NurPhoto/Getty Images, 10-11; ShutterProductions/Shutterstock, 12; Nordroden/Shutterstock, 13 (computers); Peter Hermes Furian/Shutterstock, 13 (fission); ITAR-TASS Photo Agency/Alamy Stock Photo, 14-15; Gelpi/Shutterstock, 16; Fotokon/Shutterstock, 17; Prasit Rodphan/Shutterstock, 20-21; Mikhail Markovskiy/Shutterstock, 23.

Printed in the United States of America at Corporate Graphics in North Mankato, Minnesota.

TABLE OF CONTENTS

CHAPTER 1

ACCIDENT

It was 1:00 a.m. on April 26, 1986. An explosion rocked the **nuclear power plant** in Chernobyl.

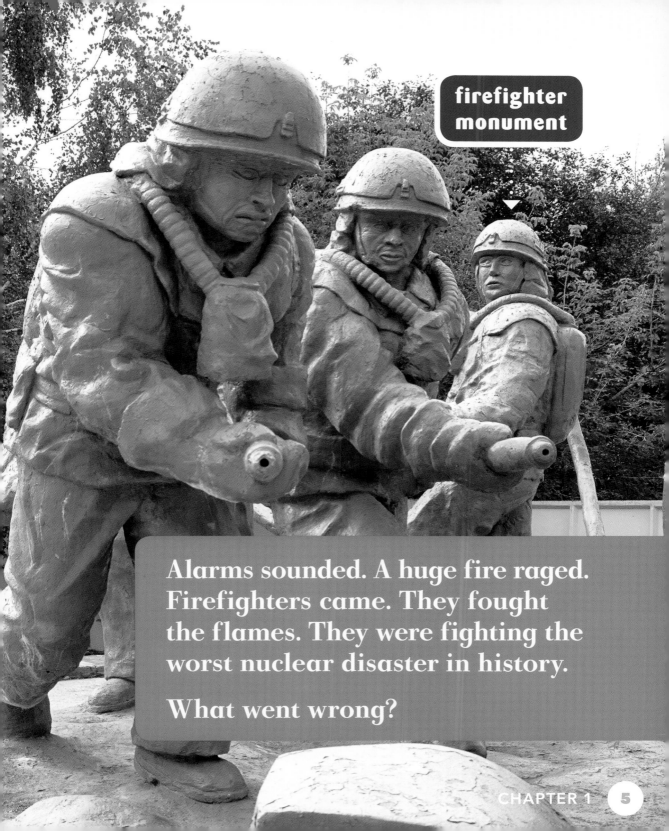

firefighter monument

Alarms sounded. A huge fire raged. Firefighters came. They fought the flames. They were fighting the worst nuclear disaster in history.

What went wrong?

Workers had run a safety test on the plant's **reactors**. They ran them at low power. But the design was bad. The reactors were not stable at low power.

Safety rules were not followed. Emergency systems had been shut off.

WHERE IS IT?

The Chernobyl plant is in Ukraine.

RUSSIA

Chernobyl •

UKRAINE

N
W ✛ E
S

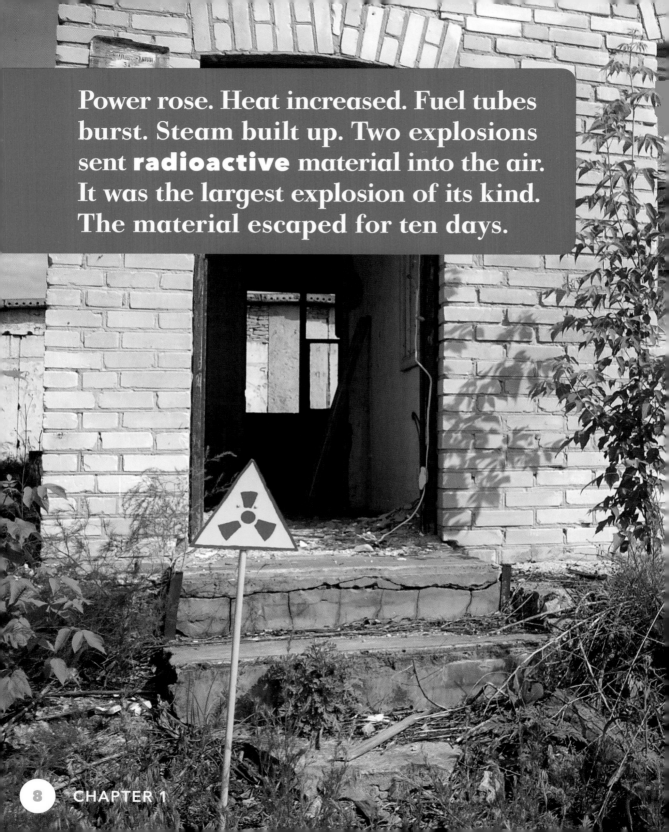

Power rose. Heat increased. Fuel tubes burst. Steam built up. Two explosions sent **radioactive** material into the air. It was the largest explosion of its kind. The material escaped for ten days.

TAKE A LOOK!

Radioactive material went into the air. The surrounding air, soil, water, plants, animals, and people were harmed by the **pollution**.

Air

Water

Soil

Plants and Animals

Two workers died right away. More than 100 workers were hurt. Within four months 28 more people died. **Radiation** made them sick.

DID YOU KNOW?

Many items give off low levels of radiation. Microwaves. Cell phones. Even the air and soil. But radiation at high levels can be bad for us. It can hurt or change our body's **cells**. It can cause cancer.

CHAPTER 2

FISSION

Nuclear plants make electricity. Other power plants burn fuel like coal or oil.

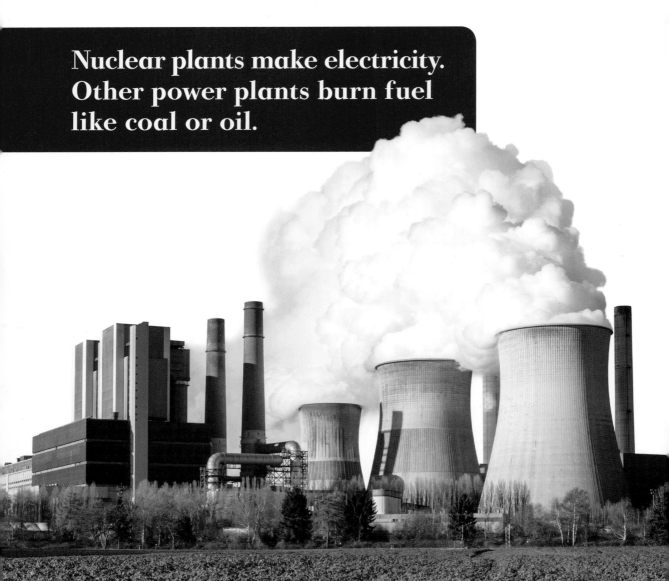

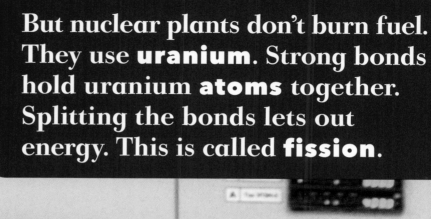

But nuclear plants don't burn fuel. They use **uranium**. Strong bonds hold uranium **atoms** together. Splitting the bonds lets out energy. This is called **fission**.

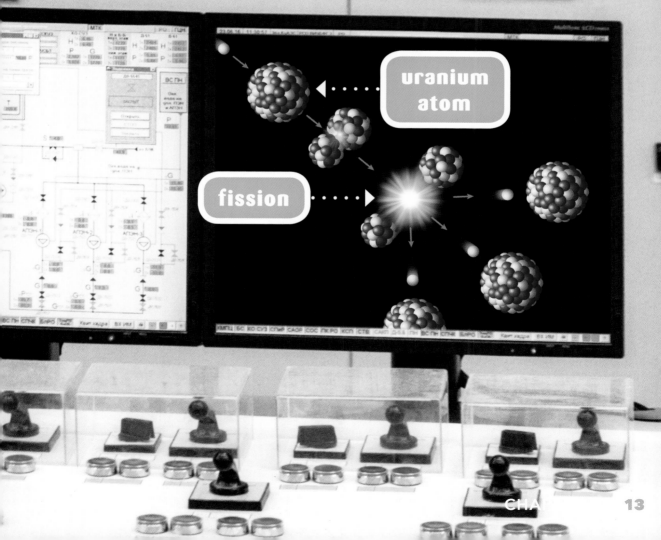

uranium atom

fission

turbine

In the plant, fission warms water. It turns to steam. Steam turns **turbines**. They spin **generators**. This makes electricity.

This process makes waste. Waste from nuclear plants is radioactive. This waste got out during the accident.

CHAPTER 3

CONTAINMENT

Most nuclear plants have **containment** buildings. They are large. They keep waste from getting out. Chernobyl's plant did not have these.

containment building

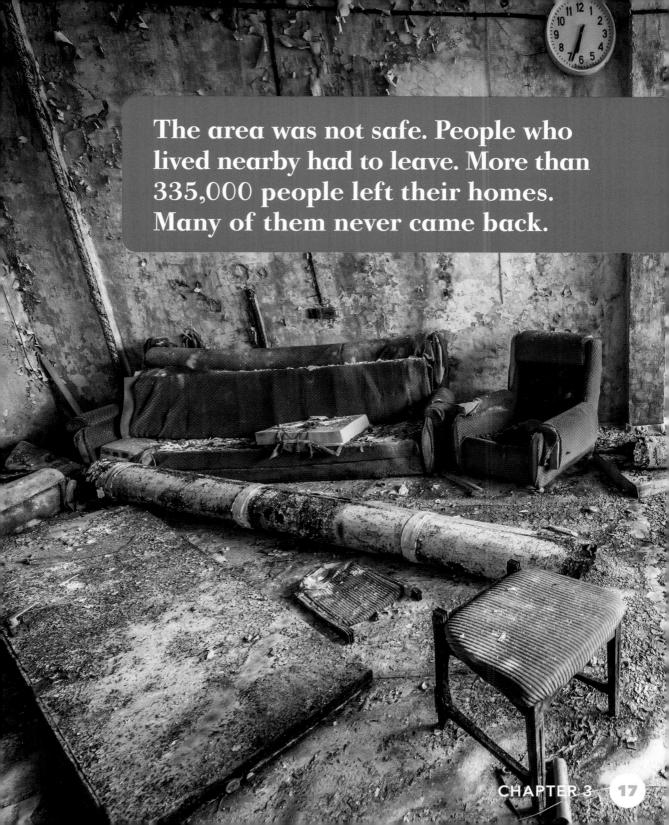

The area was not safe. People who lived nearby had to leave. More than 335,000 people left their homes. Many of them never came back.

new shelter

Workers built a shelter for the plant. But it was a temporary fix. It began to crumble. In 2016, a new shelter was built over the old one. It was the largest object people had ever moved. It should last 100 years.

People learned from the Chernobyl accident. Designs for machines were made better. Today's plants have emergency plans. If there is an accident, authorities are called immediately. People will be moved out quickly. We are better prepared to avoid nuclear disasters.

DID YOU KNOW?

Tourists can now visit Chernobyl. They are warned not to touch objects. They should not even sit on the ground. When they leave, they are checked for radiation.

ACTIVITIES & TOOLS

TRY THIS!

NUCLEAR CHAIN REACTION

How can we control nuclear reactions? By using control rods. Demonstrate how they work with this activity.

What You Need:
- dominoes
- ruler
- sturdy table

1. Arrange two straight lines of dominoes next to each other on the table.

2. Push over the front domino in one of the two lines. Watch as the dominoes fall. This row represents the nuclear chain reaction.

3. Place the ruler between two of the dominoes in the second row. Push over the front domino. Watch what happens. The dominoes should stop falling at the ruler. The ruler represents control rods in the reactor. Control rods stop or slow the chain reaction.

GLOSSARY

atoms: The smallest particles of a substance that have the chemical properties of the substance, consisting of protons, neutrons, and electrons.

cells: The basic building blocks of living things.

containment: Keeping something under control.

fission: The splitting of an atom with the release of energy.

generators: Machines that produce electricity.

nuclear power plant: A building in which electric power is generated by the process of splitting atoms.

pollution: A substance in the environment that is harmful or has poisonous effects.

radiation: A type of dangerous, powerful energy produced by nuclear reactions.

radioactive: Producing a dangerous, powerful form of energy.

reactors: Devices that contain and control nuclear chain reactions.

turbines: Devices that convert the energy of a moving fluid into rotary motion to spin generators.

uranium: A silvery-white, radioactive element mined from the ground that is used to make nuclear energy.

INDEX

TO LEARN MORE

Learning more is as easy as 1, 2, 3.

1) Go to www.factsurfer.com

2) Enter "Chernobyl" into the search box.

3) Click the "Surf" button to see a list of websites.

With factsurfer, finding more information is just a click away.